A TERRIBLE THING

Gita Ralleigh is a writer, practi
to Indian immigrant parents in ı ... ose to where
she still lives. She has been publis ... *Wasafiri*, *Bellevue Literary Review*, *The Emma Press* and *Magma*. She also teaches creative writing to science undergraduates and is completing an MSc on the intersection of literature with illness and medicine.

A Terrible Thing

Published by Bad Betty Press in 2020
www.badbettypress.com

Cover design by Amy Acre

Printed and bound in the United Kingdom

A CIP record of this book is available from the British Library.

ISBN: 978-1-913268-09-1

Gita
Ralleigh

A TERRIBLE THING

PRESS

It is a terrible thing
To be so open: it is as if my heart
Put on a face and walked into the world.

– Sylvia Plath, *Three Women*

A Terrible Thing

To Leela & Rohan

Contents

A Terrible Thing

Things break, beti, my little one. I'm sorry
I yelled and you cried, sorry for the shattered

snow globe, its fairytale plastic shards
and glycerine tears. But secretly I'm glad.

I've told you the stories, haven't I? On the path
to Nani's house, a sher stalks us. For each gulab

that blooms, a hundred kante prick small fingers.
Rainclouds, not sunbeams darken our garden,

a saap hisses from overgrown grass. For the bulbul
who sings sweet as you, daughter, somewhere

a pinjara swings from a balcony. Tiny nightingale
all I can do is fling the cage door wide, hope you fly.

Secretly, I'm glad you know how it is. To break
a thing and live, the thing forever broken.

beti daughter   *sher* tiger   *gulab* rose   *kante* thorn
saap snake   *bulbul* nightingale   *pinjara* cage

Falling

Draupadi in the *Mahābhārata*:
divine beauty, black pearl
staked in a game of dice.

What kind of hero gambles
his wife, begs forgiveness
at her hennaed feet? A crowd

of leering victors dare to strip
her bare but Krishna spares her
with a sari unspooling, endless.

See her curse and spit as her
magic silk loosens like unbound
hair. The sky is turning to ashes.

Watch her run, hear thunder drum
from tumbled footsteps. Lightning
strikes from the whites of her eyes

the air electrifies with verses.
One for every falling girl, each
pearl raining on dry earth.

love=rain

I learned that love=rain from Bollywood,
    tinted silver and black. In those old movies

studio rains stream down like an
    aria's final note. Violin strings strain

to the heights of a soprano's voice.
    Under umbrella silk and the lights

of passing cars, Nargis sings, her face
    blooms in a lover's embrace. I don't deny–

I thrill for a tabla beat of rain on the roof
    while lovemaking. Even the mizzle and spit

of London drizzle–no monsoon, too cold
    for saris. A black umbrella made bridal

canopy, beneath it, bodies collide,
    willing. Yesterday's words are undone,

our foreheads kiss. The slick tarmac mirrors
    streetlights, spills sodium galaxies at our feet.

Four Variations on Ilā and Budha in the Forest of Reeds

After Vahni Capildeo

Ilā (he/she)

Taking my arrow
from quiver, placing
tip upon taut string
I am set loose.

A wishing breaks over hard
ground. Tree roots swell
and blister. Gone are all
the horses and riders.

In lakewater
I am glass, simulacra.
Changeable as
compass needle

or new moon,
carrying Ilā
from real to who
unreels me here.

Budha (they)

Born of the moon
and faithless stars
I am that cursed prince
who lives

by night's screech and air.
I am that ghost prince,
I walk alone in crowds.
The forest leaves whisper

enchantment
or else the lakewater.
Either way, it lasts a month
on bare brown earth

our first loving.
Trees are uprooted,
rushing streams thirst.
A distant pounding of hooves.

gossip (emojis)

🤴/👸! 🤴/🤴!
🤴/👸! 🤴/🤴!

We h👂d the gossip. A coupling ❤️
changing with each 🌒
and now her belly swells 🤰
We are watching 😲
Our heads hum like spinning tops!
😲, 🤯

sarvanam (pronoun)

How sweet and all knowing
is your arrowed
moonbeam tongue.
I reel with the changing
days. Consider our
nights, sung with
starstruck limb. Life
beating down on us
as water in dry season.
Tell the learned sages
claiming man more than
woman. Tell those spinning
charms to end the spell. I'd
sacrifice lush and flowering lands
for your broken palace, give all for
this desert of shifting sands.

Sonnet for a Doll's House

An occupant of the doll's house
reports a slow outbreak of riots.

A wilderness of fists defiant,
sheets slit to slender noose.

Bloodflower memories, hurled
to paint the walls of cells.

Bright mouths unseal the spell:
taint the cries of haunted girls

telling how a doll's dismembered.
Four sprawl of light limbs left

on barebone floor, torso bereft.
Her still face unremembered.

Girl's a harp with thirteen strings
plucked and broken, still she sings.

Erzulie of the Wrongs

Lady Erzulie
erotic as crashing wave,
love as fine-milled sand,
gold dust seeding rusted hearts.

Blessed Erzulie
bind your children close,
womanhood is sanguine,
round and ripe as oranges.

Gagged Erzulie
power cleaved and spliced,
unraveled hair, mapped veins
bloody rivers, seed defiles mouth.

Red Eyed Erzulie
hold up your nascent flame,
make the old shadows dance,
strike out spiny roots and dig, dig.

Cell

She enters the cell & kneels alone to pray.
Supplication permitted only as imposed
time stretches to waves she will not resist.

Watches her lonely spirit separate from body
rise like ice upon the waters. Too much
pressure & lungs collapse. A blink of a lid

silence falls: a roof, a shelter of dreams
lifting eye's desolation. Flood this chamber
in pulsing light, it is finite as the human heart.

Diaspora:

Handful of unwanted seeds flung on a land
unforgiven. Dusky faces turned
to a painted sun. None but

sucked-up favours from crust and bones.
Our hands tapped drums, shuffled
cards of work and home.

We sung and stitched silk scraps of lives.
Coiled threads up mountains, pleated
seas to waves, crossed

with a jump. Pierce skin and a needle hurts.
How else to sew this wound? Long
mouth, gaping earth.

To thread a child's eyes shut to fear
hum songs of hope–how it blooms
watered with tears.

Anagolay, Goddess of Lost Things

Anagolay sits on the roof of the world:
    a rich man's garden thirty stories
above the city. Full grown banyans,
    roots tangling earthwards.
        Vines cloak the walls green,
        blooms sigh seeds on hot winds.

A good spot to survey the sky palaces
    slums, churches and trash heaps.
Anagolay clasps callused hands to
    knees. A name on the lips of women
        bent in kitchens, seeking what's lost
        by day: earrings, keys, eyeglasses.

Why do mortals never learn?
    All coupling is temporary.
Home never lasts. Few can bear
    truth day after day. Lost hopes
        washed to city gutters,
        drown in muddy water.

Night comes. The city is a net of light
  loss fills its dark spaces.
A woman drawing water from the
  pump lost daughters. A child
    reading by lamplight lost a mother.
    Lost boys, muzzled and prodded

roped and marched in jungle darkness.
  Lost girls crying from cages.
Anagolay! I am lost. Trace my veins
  like a leaf. Follow stem's twist
    to groundwater, touch milky root.
    Take me back to the earth.

bird, smoke, fire

how did I learn to speak
these words, like a child?

did I see in *bird*
narrow beaked intent,
a curving swoop, in
chirriyaa a whirr of flutter
and matchstick feet.

and *fire*, did I exhale
as in air and aftermath,
while *aag* rose in a pillar
of sacred flame
scorching ceilings.

once I hissed out *smoke*,
curled sibilance following
bird, tracing *baadal*.
inhaled *dhuaa* at dusk,
spiralling from *zameen*
to empty *asmaan*

I remember
nights sleeping on
rooftops and below
us the city, small fires
crying smoke. Waking,
the birds lifted us
to the broken light
of *savera*.

chirriyaa sparrow *aag* fire *baadal* cloud *dhuaa* smoke *zameen* earth
asmaan sky *savera* dawn

Birdhead

I ask the birdhead
girl in the mirror what
she really, really wants.

To peck and spit,
claw and fight–
to wildwing
at danger's beat.

She turns her head
to one-eyed profile
unblinking black.

To live now and
die whenever–
to tongue berries:
red and white,
sweet and bitter.

Shrugging, the
birdheaded girl's
shoulders are two
knifeblades.

To break blue
shell, circle city spire —
to swing needle
where I will.

Birdhead girl
wries her neck,
hearing the call
of her kind:

a sonation of
thin-feather wings,
untethered hearts
beatbeatbeat for flight.

Abhisarika

Night skies here are dark as lovers.
Black-skinned Krishna, clothed
in indigo. Bruise-lipped, love-bitten.
Night moon, fogged by heat
gold earring in peacock sky.
Night trees feathered streetlight
neon. Fluting notes curve over hills
where Radha walks, sighing beneath
a peepal tree's shivering leaves.

Princess, Abandoned

Unwanted seventh daughter, tombed
in a jewel box, thrown to deep waters.

Three golden turtles swam you ashore
to be found by fisherfolk, Princess.

Doomed to abandon by royal parents,
loyal when you seek and find them

near death. You prise your heart open
like a casket. Inside, only love. Hearing

of miracles, fearing nothing, you steer
by pole star's cold light to the world

of spirits. Take any chore: dig fields,
wash floors, scrub the dead's dirty linen,

watch rain flood upon the earth. The
old man guarding the fountain of life

makes you his slave and wife. Seven
years later, you steal the water and fly

to revive the King and Queen who left
you dying. Lift the cup to their grey lips,

feel a faint skitter of pulse, see blind
eyes blink alive. Turn away and leave.

Don't ask them why or if they grieved.
Raise rainbow sleeves wide and walk

a graveyard path to the land of night,
where the spirits love you, or might.

churel

return to me
on misty nights.
as grief branches
to madness.
trees walk paths
whispering names
in leaf-tongues.

a shadow drifting
at cat's pace
silver eyes fixed
on the clouded
moon, penumbra
flooding milk to
spinning stars.

a night of broken
bangles, blood
pooling on earth.
body turned stone
marigolds placed
on closed eyelids
and in my dreams

birdsong brings
news of the dead.
on bare ground
a split fruit
the spilt seed
crows pecking
at ripe flesh.

a *churel* is the revenant spirit of a woman who dies in childbirth.

Grandmother Tiger

On the seventh hour of the seventh day of the seventh
month comes the hour of the birds stifling their clamour

Here East Wind meets West Wind and stills Here is the hill
of white rice laid in the courtyard pecked at by silent crows

Here a robe of midnight silk stitched for you Grandmother
three white cranes in flight across each sleeve Here I await

the nip of your ivory fangs crushbone kisses swished from
your snaking tail The three-footed raven yarls your coming

nine-tailed fox brushes the swept earth Here the moonhare
springs from desolate sky at your bidding Three bluebirds tattooed

on my wrist cut free to circle your nine-star crown pluck the
white strands for nests Here Grandmother Tiger we lie down

to sleep Here where the dust is cool A thousand years shall pass
in a cricket's chirp between thump of bamboo staff on the ground

between the tintinnabulation of frogs Here the immortal fruit of
words ripen and fall I will tear them open between your snarls

Black Winged Butterfly

We dine at eight but *ah!*
how days grow long here,
the shadows strong.
Their women grind and
chatter at cock-crow,
beating linens white,
only to bloody again.
All I long for is *watersaltmilk*,
not bread to break with her

whose clawfeet skulk
under my husband's table.
Deerhide gloves sheathe talons
black hair interrogates
a leadpaint face.
Wings of obsidian
beating at her back,
she seeks to befriend me
but does not smile,
lays a glovehand on mine.

Thin shoulders twitching
a nighttime yen to fly,
skirts strung with clattering
flints, she leans close
tells me they are hers,
the infants I lost. *Safe.*
Lifts silver fork, stabs deerheart.
Raising it to red maw, she
sighs long with pleasure.

Inanna, Queen of the Desert.

Inanna looks into the mirage. Straightens her
crown of thorns. Washes grit from her eyes, wipes
red dirt from her lips. *Babe, you're sexy,* she tells her
reflection. *Unstoppable. You will get all you deserve.*

Inanna lines her eyes with kohl, oils hallowed
limbs, brushes rippling hair. Dressed in denim,
blue water on desert sand, she walks out under
heat that makes birds drop from the sky.

Enki's place is by the lake where cedars grow.
Hearing Inanna's coming he panics:
tells his servants to clean up, buy buttercakes,
the vintage wine she likes and plenty of it.

Inanna sprawls in a silk robe, swigging red
from a bronze chalice. Feels right at home. *Enki!*
How about a drinking game? Enki's a happy drunk.
You know why I'm here. Inanna tells him *I want it all!*

From under the table, Enki grants Inanna all
she desires. Heroism and power, good and evil,
mourning and rejoicing. A fire spark, war and victory,
how to plunder rebel lands. Inanna wants more.

Inanna wants craft and kingship, priestess and priest.
Strife and counsel, the standard and quiver, the arts
of sexual intercourse, music and song. Inanna loads it
all in the Boat of Heaven, drives off to pick up her girl

Ninshubur. Enki sobers up to find Inanna has
taken everything. He sends guards to kill Inanna
sends monstrous men and giants to hunt Inanna
who is only a girl, Inanna who is unstoppable.

Inanna drags her haul home to the city. People
worship her here, call her the Queen of Heaven.
Centuries go by, reluctantly Inanna grows old.
She lives with her girl Ninshubur by the lake

gulping wine, playing online poker. Inanna's
power is a young girl's game. She weathers
beneath the desert sun like Enki's bronze chalice.
Buried in dust, made glittering by sudden rain.

Sisters of The Moon

Take a mirror. Come daughter,
skies are clear, stars glister.
Tilt the mirror. I'll tell of
our fickle sisters of the moon.

New Moon
Artemis demands her right to bare
legs. To wield bow and arrow, roam
mountains, forests and wild places.
To keep eternal virginity, transform
stray men to trees or rutting stags.

First Quarter
Selene, sister of Helios and Eos.
Arcing black skies in a chariot,
silver crescent crown of horns.
Selene takes Endymion asleep,
births fifty mortal beauties.

Full Moon
Luminous Dewi Ratih, stalked by
Kala Rau. Begs Vishnu to behead
the giant creep, who sips the nectar
of immortality. His yawn eclipses Dewi,
she leaps at his neck, sickle drawn.

Third Quarter
Arianrhod refuses her son a name,
weapons, wife–all that makes a man.
Her son takes a bride of flowers. Fool
doesn't know how a girl blooms: with
thornprick, sapstain and owl's hoot.

A spell to keep off harm, daughter.
Hold a mirror to moonlight, cup
circle in palm. Call upon our
clawed sisters of the night.

The Wind God's Wife

I knew he was *wind* when he
came on a breath, *god* when

he spun atoms into storms
stripped my greenery bare.

He never stayed long, headed
off like a train, pulling away

with a whistle and sigh. Left
me waiting on station platforms

rain's swift teeth hammering
black rails. Blood scattered

to dust and iron, his magnet
pull gone. Where he'd won me

between lips and cunt wholly
vacant, a hollow for the one

within who'd begun a terror
of kicking and tumbling. His

son, born to dream distances
wild as the god of four winds.

Prayer to Oshun

We had no gold, no coral
amber, citrine, tourmaline.
Flung asunder across tilting grey.
Shackled, chained, helpless.
Far from your holy rivers, no offerings for
Oshun who knows poverty and despair.
Oshun, powerful child of rivers.
Oshun, goddess of beauty and love.
Now we offer all good things to you
Candied yams, honey, worked gold.
Our children, our children's children.
You heard our prayer, not forsaking us
And we lived
We lived.

how to be a minority woman

When cooking, pound a myriad of spices.
Let them gild your fingertips. Embroider

tiny stitches, intricate flowers. Make spells
of bright threads against words that prick

your skin. Walk with grace, wind scarf on
languorous neck. Wear silver chimes, gold

tremors. Lower curtains of gleaming black
hair, conceal a yearning to be torn aside.

Keep your tone pitched low. Quietude is
an excellent thing in a minority woman.

On no account ever raise your voice.
Demand nothing, play shy as a small

bird and you may peck at our discarded
crumbs. Unlike us, the fewer you are

the better. Best to remain a pleasantly
exotic mystery. Birth dark-eyed children

if you must but not too many. Don't place
your painted toes over the line dividing

undeserving minority from deserving
majority. Trust me, it will not end well.

Time's Up, Mr Wolf

After Elina Chauvet's Zapatos Rojos

Red shoes walking pavement and street, empty of feet.
Steelcaps, stilettos, plimsolls, pumps. Scarlet, carmine,
ruby, blood. High heels click the lead: *one step, two step,*
thump, thump, thump. The smallest shoes belong
to girls raised by wolves. *Tonight* the girls say.
We wear our wolfsuits and make trouble of only one kind.
One step, two step, three step, four. Slide on marble floors
kick in steel prison doors. *What's the time Mr Wolf?*
Mr Wolf skulks. Gut hung in furskin, spit loops from jowl.
Mr Wolf howls as the red shoes split and gouge!
What's the time Mr Wolf? Mr Wolf cries foul, matted pelt
studded with welts. But the red shoes are not done.
Red shoes walking uptown, stamping down the rhyme
one step two step. Mr Wolf! What's the time?

Five Rivers

like the Roman, I seem to see the River Tiber
foaming with much blood

Enoch Powell, 1968

I come from a land of five rivers known
to the ancients. Punj-aab, or five waters:
Jhelum, Chenab, Ravi, Beas and Sutlej.
Slower than tides, red as dying suns.

Five tributaries meet as fingers
on a hand to form the mighty Indus.
In the Rig-Veda, India's rivers are
female: Ganga, Sarasvati and Yamuna.

All but the Indus, his current spumed
with a bull's power, rushing waters
a speeding war chariot. India was
named for the land east of the Indus

but at Partition, a line severed Punjab.
Five fingers seeped blood. Corpses
silted the Jhelum where Alexander once
battled Porus. Starless waters flowed

dark in this divided land of mine. A body
is our first home and last, we know its
coursing arteries and slow veins as
a land knows rivers. Let them flood.

Commandments

Let us never again
cast the widow
upon the pyre.

Let us agree
not to drown
the witch.

Let us no longer
abandon babes in
churchyards.

Let us cheer on
the unruliest of
daughters.

Let us blame
our mothers
no more.

Let us worship
every whore
as sacred being.

Let us be guided
by the intellects of
young girls.

Let us live as
wise women, who
rule the world.

Saraswati / Benzaiten

You are your own self,
adrift on white-feather swan,
goddess of all that
shimmers, flows like the river:
sweet music, poetry, wisdom–

those arts that travel
to far distant lands, crossing
borders. Your many
hands clasp lute, prayer beads, holy
book as you travel East; your

lotus throne passes
below the red temple gate,
the abode of birds.

Sylvia by the Ganges

what she remembers

how the walls moved inwards/ how the dark came early and left without saying goodbye/ pipes birthed ice with a rattle/ a banshee kettle keened death / spirit escaping as steam / nothing of spring/ not a bird or flower or leaf/ winter had tired of her/ twisted his cruel mouth / she was tired of her own self/

what she sees

blinking she raises a head/ shorn close as a newborn/ stretches gangly limbs/ long toes trace water/ forested slopes cradle her green/ high peaks lift bearded heads to heaven/ river rushes/ brown and silver maned horses/ white calf on the far bank/ child leading it to the rising waters/ widowed of her own self/

she thinks of the blue lotus/ flowering only at night/ rounds her mouth to an unfamiliar chant/ thinks of the morning star/ closes her suffering eyes/

Notes

Abhisarika is a name for Radha as wandering lover.

Anagolay is the Filipino (Tagalog) goddess of lost things.

Arianrhod in Welsh legend placed a geis or curse on her son to have no name, weapons or wife. With a magician, he makes a woman from flowers, Blodeuwedd, who is later turned into a screech owl.

Artemis is the Greek goddess of the hunt and wild animals.

Bari Gongju or Abandoned Princess was the seventh daughter of a king, abandoned by her parents at birth. She is the first shaman in Korean legend, helping spirits of the dead to pass to the other world.

Benzaiten is the Japanese goddess of water, music, words and eloquence.

Dewi Ratih is a lunar goddess worshipped in Java and Bali.

Draupadi is the heroine of the Indian epic, the *Mahābhārata*.

Erzulie is a Haitan Voudou spirit or loa with different forms including Erzulie Dantor, or Erzulie of the Wrongs.

Grandmother Tiger or Queen Mother of the West in Chinese Taoist beliefs guarded the tree of immortality and was often portrayed with a tiger's teeth and tail.

Ilā in Hindu myth was a prince who entered an enchanted forest in which every male became female. She married Prince Budha, uniting the lunar and solar dynasties.

Inanna was the Sumerian goddess of love, war and power also known to the Babylonians as Ishtar.

Itzpapalotl, known as the Obsidian, Clawed or Black Winged Butterfly was an Aztec goddess who ruled over Tamoanchan, a paradise where babies who died in infancy lived.

Oshun is a Yoruba orisha of love and fertility also worshipped in Santeria, Candomblé and Voudou.

Radha is the consort of Krishna, the avatar of Vishnu in Hinduism.

Saraswati is the Hindu goddess of poetry, music and the arts. Her vehicle or vahana is a white swan. Via the spread of Buddhism she became syncretized with the Japanese goddess Benzaiten.

Selene of Greek myth is sister of Helios the sun and Eos the dawn. After she fell in love with handsome shepherd Endymion, Zeus granted him eternal youth.

Acknowledgements

Thank you to all the poetry deities who saw this work at an early stage: Pascale Petit, George Szirtes, Rishi Dastidar, Zeina Hashem Beck, Nisha Ramayya & Shivanee Ramlochan.

Thanks to Emma Dai'An Wright of *The Emma Press*, who gave me my first ever poetry publication. I am so grateful to Anita Pati & Sarala Estruch for being inspirational sisters in verse and to Farhana Shaikh of *The Asian Writer* for providing opportunities to learn from the best poets.

Many prayers, offerings & duas for the poets, teachers, poetry lovers and small presses out there doing the work.

And a huge, huge thank you to the absolute dream team of Jake Wild Hall & the brilliant Amy Acre of Bad Betty. I feel unbelievably lucky to have worked with you both.

Bird, Smoke, Fire first appeared in The Brown Orient, *Anagolay, Goddess of Lost Things* in Liminality and *Birdhead* in Magma Poetry.

Four Variations on Ilā and Budha in the Forest of Reeds was inspired by Vahni Capildeo's astonishing *Four Departures from 'Wulf and Eadwacer'*.

Other titles by Bad Betty Press

2020

poems for my FBI agent
Charlotte Geater

War Dove
Troy Cabida

Animal Experiments
Anja Konig

Sylvanian Family
Summer Young

bloodthirsty for marriage
Susannah Dickey

At the Speed of Dark
Gabriel Àkámọ

Rheuma
William Gee

Field Notes on Survival
Edited by Amy Acre and Jake Wild Hall

2019

While I Yet Live
Gboyega Odubanjo

She Too Is a Sailor
Antonia Jade King

Blank
Jake Wild Hall

The Body You're In
Phoebe Wagner

Raft
Anne Gill

And They Are Covered in Gold Light
Amy Acre

Alter Egos
Edited by Amy Acre and Jake Wild Hall

No Weakeners
Tim Wells

After the Stabbing
Zena Edwards

The Lives of the Female Poets
Clare Pollard

Give Thanks / for Shukri
Amaal Said

South of South East
Belinda Zhawi

2018

In My Arms
Setareh Ebrahimi

The Story Is
Kate B Hall

I'm Shocked
Iris Colomb

Ode to Laura Smith
Aischa Daughtery

The Pale Fox
Katie Metcalfe

TIGER
Rebecca Tamás

The Death of a Clown
Tom Bland

The Dizziness Of Freedom
Edited by Amy Acre and Jake Wild Hall

2017

Solomon's World
Jake Wild Hall

Unremember
Joel Auterson

Ingram Content Group UK Ltd.
Milton Keynes UK
UKHW010644270723
425883UK00004B/263